The Duck Farted

Poems and Drawings by Chester Black

Coldworthy
Writers Guild LLC

Copyright (May 21,2025) By Chester Black

All rights reserved. No part of this book may be reproduced, transmitted, or stored in an information retrieval system in any form or by any means, graphic, electronic, including photocopying, taping, and recording, without the prior written permission from the publisher, except where permitted by law.

ISBN: 979-8-9994902-0-9

Becoming a poet can be tricky

Unless you have a muse like my Mickey

She encouraged me to get started

By writing poems about someone who farted

While reciting his poem "My Little Rubber Ducky" a 4-year-old laughed and said "The duck farted". All the other children laughed, and explained that it was the kid in the tub that farted, rubber ducks can't fart. The 4-year-old joined in on the laughter Thus, the title.

Contents

Page #

1 Never Say Fart

3. A Boy Who Farts

4 Pig Fart

5 Little Bridie

6 Polite

9 Bean Mobile

11 Bean Perfumed

13 Bees

14 Ornithologist

15 The Legend

17 Bomb Squad

19 Old Man in a Boot

20 Brimstone

21 Breaking Wind

23 Cleaning

24 Write a Poem

25 The Explorer

27 Fertilizer

28 Fleeting Warmth

29 Floated Away

30 Frosty Mustache

31 Fred Exploded

33 Grandma's Toots

34 Good Morning

35 I Can't Stand It

37 I Did Feel Ill

38 Late Night

39 I Run Every Day

40 Impolite to Explode

41 It Was You

42 Jack and John

43 Little Cherub

45 My Little Rubber Ducky

46 Morning Meditation

47 Mom

48 In the Air

49 Oscar

50 The Phantom

51 The Sneeze

53 Point at Your Brother

55 Pull My Finger

56 Bird Bath

57 School Band

58 Mary's Sheep

59 Grandpa's Lament

60 I'm Tired

61 Thunderous Beans

63 Treats

64 Teacher Said

65 Bird Feeder

66 Grandpa Wakes Up

67 Commode-cracker

68 The Ghost

69 Guilty Blush

71 Noisy Diet

Never Say Fart

In a civil conversation
your words need always be polite
so, you must now learn
which are wrong and which are right

When talking of indigestion
and effects that it can cause
there are proper words
and others that give pause

A poof, a toot, or breaking wind
would be a good place to start
even more polite is flatulence
but you must never, ever, say---fart

A Boy Who Farts

There was a lad
who was always sad
until he met perfection

No longer coy
he was filled with joy
he worked to win her affection

He sent bouquets
and poems of praise
hoping that's how romance starts

She said although flattered
what really mattered
"I could never love a boy who farts".

Pig Fart

His smile is enigmatic
he's as proud as he can be
for his fart was not only loud
but one everyone could see

enigmatic; puzzling or mysterious

Little Birdie

Little birdie on my sill

how I love the song you trill

when you turn to fly and swoop

please don't leave behind a poop

Trill; singing two notes

Polite

While everyone farts, that fact is clear
some are silent and some you can hear

It's never good-mannered to fart in a crowd
especially if you are prone to farts that are loud

Those who fart silently think themselves civilized
while loud farters are constantly criticized

The loud farter says tooting is elemental
be they cut on purpose or passed accidental

While everyone farts, that fact is clear
a polite farter farts, only when ... no one is near

Bean Mobile

My teacher said if you dream anything
and wake and work you can make it real
that night I dreamt of the coolest car
it was the first fart powered Bean Mobile

I dreamt it was the fastest car
with a lightning bolt as yellow as the sun
I never drove it to school
only after dinner for fun

To make sure it had lots of power
mother would always do her part
she gave me a plate of beans for dinner
it was my job to supply the fart

I never knew where I might go
or when I might get back
mother worried the car would lose power
so, she packed a can of beans in a sack

I woke and knew I had to start working
to make it real like the teacher taught
so, I asked my mother to fix beans for dinner
I said I would need to eat an awful lot

Bean Perfumed

I know the nicest little boy
that anyone has ever seen
he doesn't have a single bad habit
except for eating too many beans

He eats baked beans for breakfast
and refried beans for lunch
a big bowl of bean soup for dinner
and between on green beans he'll munch

His smile is forever pleasant
and he is always well groomed
but people try to avoid him
because he is bean perfumed

Bees

Do bees think it's good luck
      or a disaster
That when they fart,
      they fly much faster

Ornithologist

Grandpa wanders from the picnic in the park
saying he is looking for a ruby throated lark

But it is not the love of ornithology in his heart
he is just looking for a quiet place to fart

ornithology; the study of birds

The Legend

He was quite the legend
for making noises rude
the boys called him a hero
the girls said he was crude

Every school day after lunch
where he ate beans to his fill
he would let out giant farts
that may be echoing still

But to prove himself an expert
winning any rude noise contest
he would demonstrate his skills
by belching on request

Bomb Squad

The tension grows
pressure is unbearable
your body knows
these farts will be terrible

You've a sweaty grin
as you hold them in
and start to get dizzy
as you race to the privy

Relief comes at last
but your plan was flawed
someone heard the blast
and called the bomb squad

Old Man in a Boot

There was an old man
 who lived in a boot
he ate so many beans
 he'd constantly toot

Beans and eggs for breakfast
 lunch of bean chowder
bean burritos for dinner
 made his toots even louder

Brimstone

The hint of brimstone

after a thunderous boom

let's everyone know

I had beans at noon

Brimstone; also called sulfur; a rock that smells like sewage, rotten eggs or farts

Breaking Wind

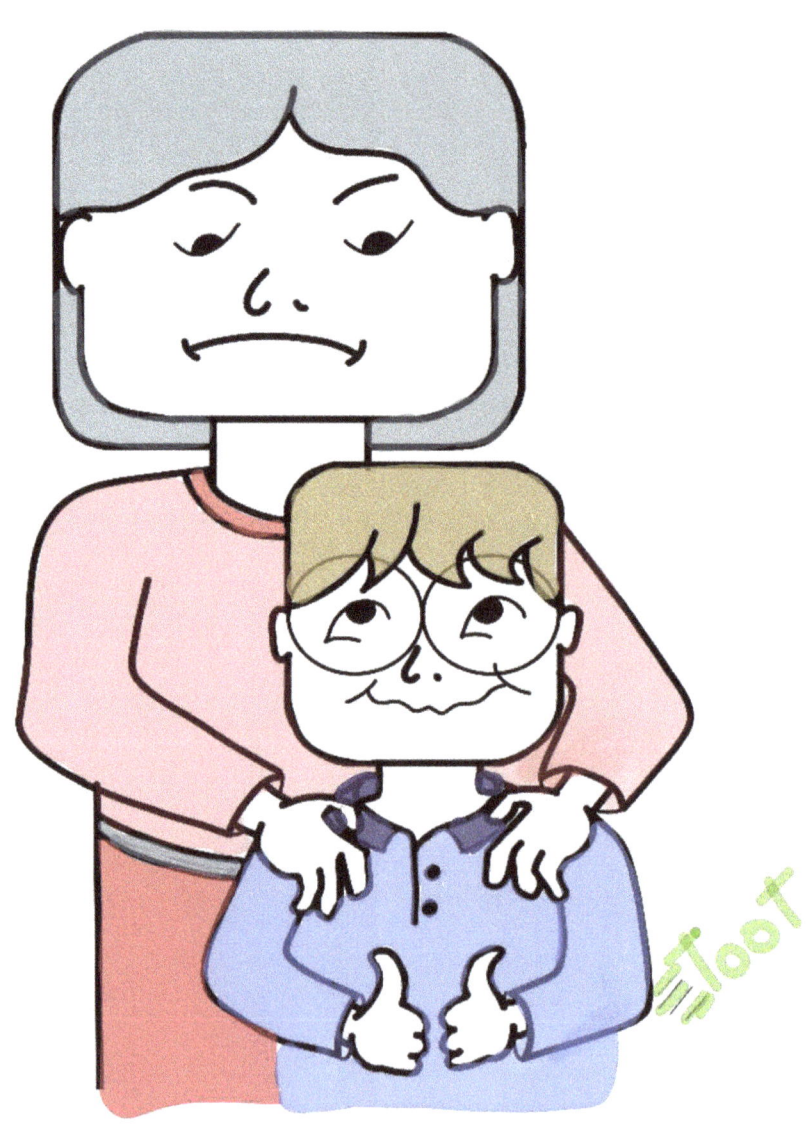

I knew a four-year-old lad
Whose mother said was never bad

She always expected the highest standards
and tried her best to teach him manners

Coat in the closet on a hanger
count to ten before showing anger

Always be honest when playing games
never call other people names

Comb your hair before you go
noses are only meant to blow

He'd do his best he avowed
to always make his mother proud

But his mother was still often chagrined
for he could not stop breaking wind

Cleaning

I clean the counter
I mop the floor
I scrub the sink
I straighten the drawer

After all my hard work
you break my heart
for you walk right in
sit down and fart

Write a Poem

Write a poem that's lighthearted
include someone who loudly farted

Recite it and discover what comes after

is the simple joy of children's laughter

The Explorer

Mother asked "Once you are grown
what work will you do, being on your own?"

He said "An explorer I've always wanted to be
to travel the world, and cross the sea"

She asked "With so much of the world already
        discovered
what mysteries are left to be uncovered?

All the highest mountains have been climbed
deep ocean submarines have been designed"

Her son answered "But no one has written catalogs
of all the different animal's fogs.

Do penguins' farts fall to the ground frozen?
when thawed do they smell like fish or the ocean?

Are lions' farts as loud as their roars?
do hibernating bears fart between snores?"

Mother said "With so many world secrets already
        revealed
imagination is important to be in the exploration
        field"

Fertilizer

Mary always eats a bean burrito
along with a taco combo
but after that wherever Mary goes
she is afraid a toot might blow

After lunch at school one day
everyone wrinkled their noses
Mary said she just saw the gardener
putting fertilizer on the roses

Manure; fertilizer made from cow, horse or chicken poop

Fleeting Warmth

I'm bundled against the cold

crossing the arctic landscape

straining hard my farts to hold

for I know they can't escape

A few more feet ahead I slog

against the wind that's beating

working hard to hold the toot's fog

knowing any warmth would be fleeting

Floated Away

Uncle Joe loved to eat beans
he could never eat enough it seems

Saying they're healthy and keep you thinner
he ate them for breakfast lunch and dinner

Uncle Joe said that he had to exclude
having to fart, for that would be rude

But he kept eating beans every day
he ate them until he floated away

Frosty Mustache

The old man's mustache got frosty
with every breath he drew
for winter quickly freezes hot air
that's why his pants are frosty too

Fred Exploded

There once was a pumpkin
by the name of Fred
who didn't want to be a pie
but a Jack-o-lantern instead

He knew if he grew
all wholesome and sweet
the family who picked him
would think he was good to eat

Fred came up with a plan
to make himself no good for eating
so, he could have lots of fun
being part of trick or treating

When Fred started growing
he thought it would be smart
to live with the beans
then he'd smell like a fart

When Halloween came
Fred's wish would begin
for little Suzy gave him
a big Jack-o-lanterny grin

But not all dreams come true
best plans are sometimes eroded
for after living a life with beans
when she lit his candle ... **Fred exploded**

Grandma's Toots

Grandpa is known

by all far and wide

for farts both loud and violent

Grandma is known

as proper and dignified

for the toots she has are silent

Good Morning

Some days Grandpa wakes up

works hard to drag himself out of bed

on those mornings his heart is filled with dread

Some days Grandpa wakes up

sure with every problem he will cope

on those mornings his heart is filled with hope

Most days Grandpa wakes up

starts his morning just like you and me

he waddles into the bathroom to fart and pee

I Can't Stand It

I have gas that's ceaseless
and flatulence galore
I'm a farting factory
I can't stand it any more

My stomach rumbles
and sometimes roars
I'm a regular calliope
I can't stand it any more

My friends are impatient
my family's deplored
I'm embarrassing myself
I can't stand it any more

I stay in the bathroom
behind the locked door
I'm becoming a hermit
I can't stand it any more

With body always bloated
a stomach always sore
I'm going to start a new life
I won't eat beans any more

Calliope; a small organ usually played at a circus
Hermit; a person who lives alone, away from other people

I Did Feel Ill

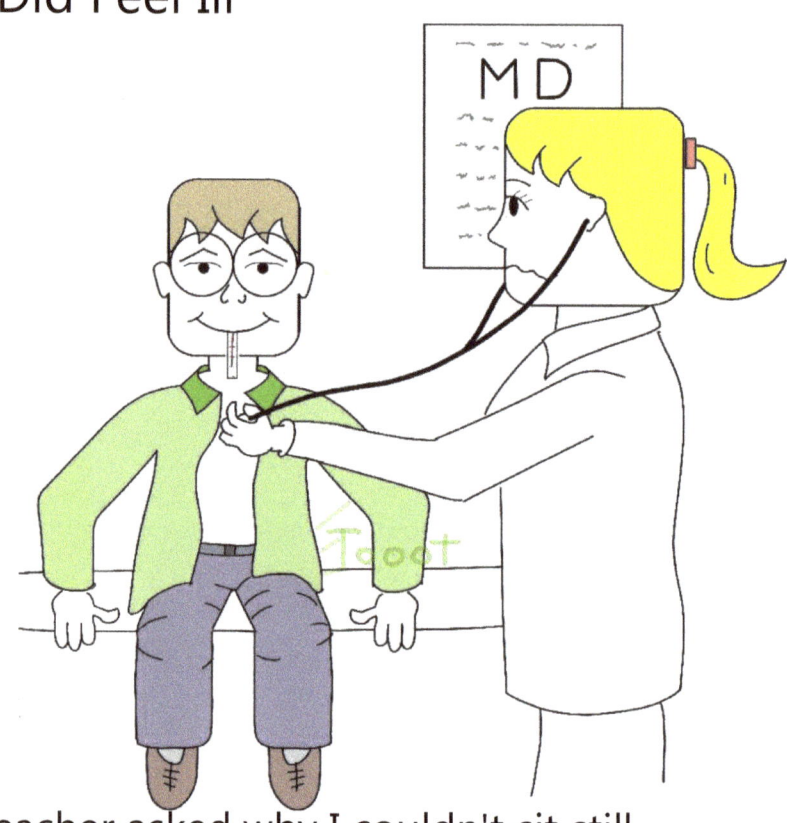

Teacher asked why I couldn't sit still

then insisted I stop squirming

when I said I really did feel ill

she said that needed confirming

The doctor found I had no fever

there was nothing wrong with my heart

but she became a believer

when I let out a giant fart

Late Night

I woke up late last night
I thought I had to pee
but all I really had to do
is set the fart in me free

I Run Every Day

I eat a healthy high fiber diet
I run a few miles every day
I'm cashing in on the benefits
while those following me have to pay

Impolite to Explode

I sat at the table
I began to fret
I really had to fart
I broke out in a sweat

Farts are never polite
with guests in your abode
but it's also not acceptable
for your stomach to explode

    Abode; another word for house

It Was You!!

I know for a fact
it wasn't me
and there is no one else
as far as I can see

The innocence you proclaim
I must thoroughly dispute
for since it wasn't mine
it had to be your toot

Jack and John

Jack and John were twins
only their mother could tell apart
for one would frown and the other grin
when one would toot and the other fart

Little Cherub

His little sister is so sweet
no one ever expects deceit
but her brother knows her shame
for he gets her share of the blame

He has to put away her toys
Is scolded for her late-night noise
but he felt he must protest
when for her farts he was asked to confess

Because she has a cherub's smile
it is easy for her to hide her guile
so, no one had ever refuted
when she said "It wasn't me that tooted"

Cherub; angel
Guile; lies or dishonestly fooling someone

My Little Rubber Ducky

My little rubber ducky
floats quietly in the tub
until suddenly surrounded
by bubbles blub-blub

Morning Meditation

This morning, we shared
our time in meditation
serenely and silently
until your flatulation

Mom

My dog has been known
to let out a smelly groan

My cat has now and then
omitted fumes that offend

My dad thinks he is stealthy
while releasing air unhealthy

But one fact can't be disputed
My mom has never tooted

In the Air

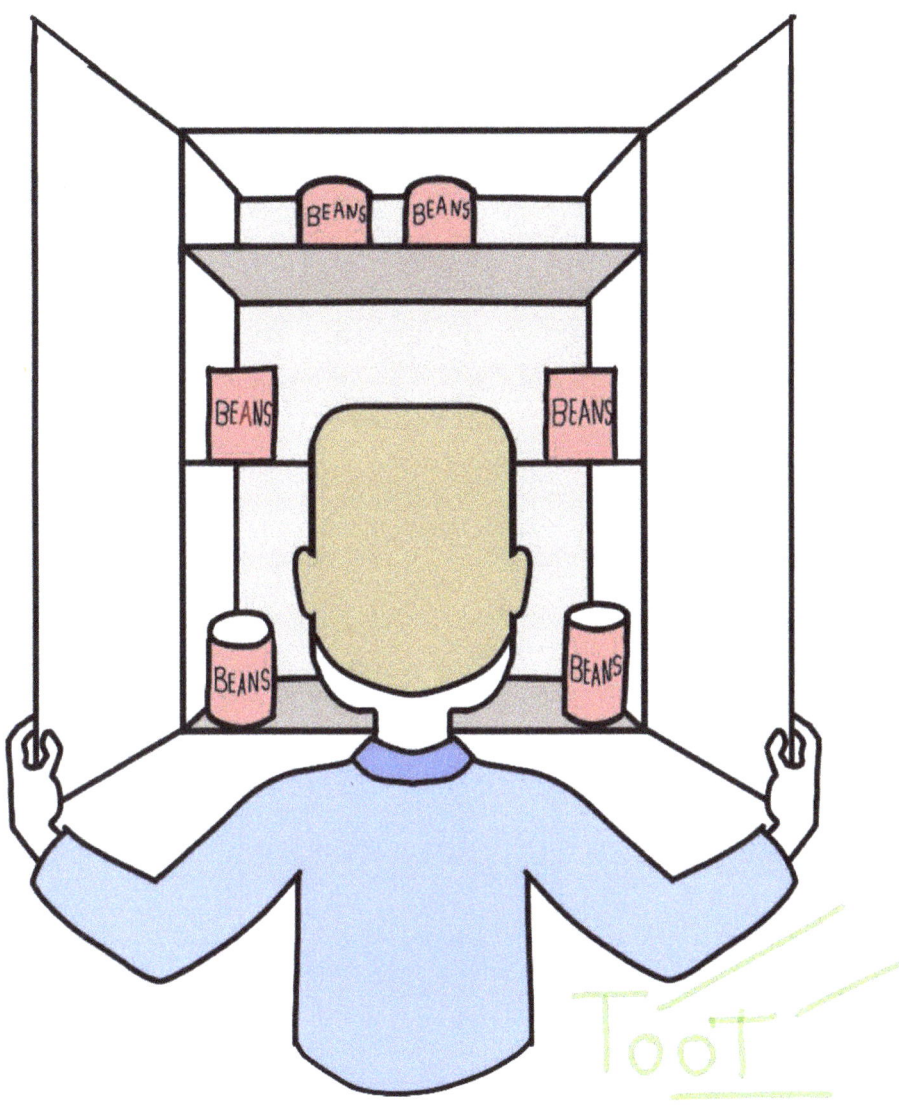

The harsh winter has been long
the cupboards are close to bare
with only beans left to eat
that's not spring in the air

Oscar

Good old Oscar
is a fine watch dog
barking out the window
at every squirrel and frog

He knows his duties
always does his part
I just wish that his bark
wasn't echoed with a fart

The Phantom

I love cabbage
I think beans are a treat
and like the old adage
you are what you eat

I live with the shame
I'm the vile perpetrator
I'm the phantom unnamed
Of ... the empty elevator

The Sneeze

I wanted to
but it wouldn't be proper
also, I'd embarrass my wife
and my daughter

To find the right time
or just the right spot
isn't that easy
in the middle of a shop

So, I asked to be excused
and from them I departed
went out to the car
where I promptly ... sneezed

Point at Your Brother

It is rude to belch in public
or sneeze out loud
but it's even more unforgivable
to fart in a crowd

When you are told by nature
it's time to make a rude sound
you need to hold it in
until a proper place is found

You may search high and low
or try scurrying behind a tree
but on the top of your list
should be to find a privy

Luck is not always with you
and to delay would make you suffer
so, before the heads all turn
you need to point at your brother

Privy: bathroom

Pull My Finger

Grandpa asked
    "Will you pull my finger"
Grandma said
    "If you do don't linger"

Bird Bath?

As the sparrow drank peacefully
a robin suddenly arrived
jumped in and started bathing
to which the sparrow cried

"This water was sparkling clean
tasted just fine and dandy
you've used it for a bathtub
now it tastes like robin fanny"

School Band

The school band
marches in long rows
so just who farted
no one knows

Mary's Sheep

Mary had a little sheep
they were never seen apart
everyone their distance would keep
for each would too often fart

It followed her to school from home
the room was filled with thunder
when asked who played the skunk trombone
they pointed at each other

Grandpa's Lament

My back is out
I lie like a log
I can't even escape
my own fart's fog

I'm Tired

Too tired to think

too tired to talk

too tired to sleep

too tired to walk

what is a person to do

when your even too tired to doo-doo

Thunderous Beans

I am what's called a foody
    that can't be denied
For I love every culinary style
    that I have ever tried

Presented with the peasant food
    of Tuscany
I've been accused of nothing short
    of gluttony

And if offered delicious lobster
    from the shores of Maine
I'll fill myself and only be stopped
    by my stomach pain

But there is something magical
    about Southwestern cuisines
I don't know if it's the spices I love
    or the thunderous beans

cuisine; the style or kind of cooking
Tuscany; an area in Italy know for good food
gluttony; the sin of overeating

Treats

I filled my bird-feeder
with beans for their treats
now I am waiting for
the toots between the tweets

The teacher told the class
it's impolite to toot
but she couldn't mean me
for my toots are mute

Mute; silent

Bird Feeder

I filled my bird-feeder
with beans for the bird
now I swear that those
weren't all tweets that I heard

Grandpa Wakes Up

Every morning that I wake

is a gift right from the start

after stretching to relieve my back ache

I greet the day with a fart

Commode-cracker

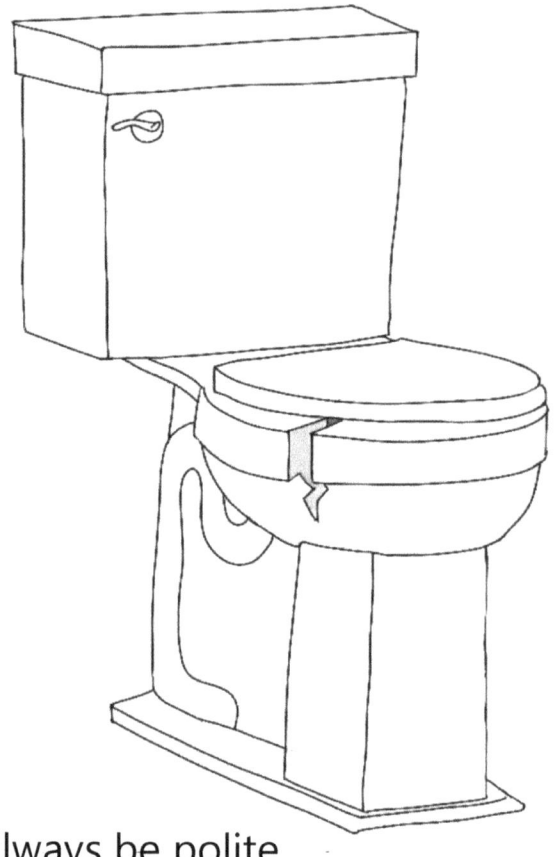

Mother said I must always be polite
good manners were consistently expected
And whenever I forgot what was right
she would make sure I was cordially corrected

She thought farting in public was the worst sin
saying anyone doing it is just a slacker
But I said if all those little farts were held in
in the bathroom I'd release a commode-cracker

The Ghost

I told my sister our house is haunted
by a very unusual ghost
he's sometimes here at night
but it's after dinner he comes the most

He does not boo or scare us
or use the typical spooky arts
but I know when he is in the room
for he toots silent ghostly farts

Guilty Blush

Susy always correct and sedate
carefully watched what she ate

All her meals where very lean
never a sugary snack in between

For that reason, she was confused
when for farting, she was accused

It hurt her pride to even think
of being suspect of farts that stink

She said her brother had the means
for he constantly dined on beans

He protested that this time he was blameless
but the guilty party would go nameless

With her deception she almost got away clean
but on her face a guilty blush could be seen

Noisy Diet

The teacher told Cris he must be quiet
Cris said the noise was from his diet
he'd eaten his fill and then some more
all those beans made his stomach roar
although his stomach was very stressed
he promised that he would do his best
he tried hard to keep his stomach still
and that's when he started feeling ill

His long silent fart was unexpected
but one those around him soon detected
Sally's eyes began to tear
Joey's face was full of fear
Mary's eyes started to spin around
Nelson was wearing a painful frown
the teacher face showed her grief
while on Cris's face was only relief

www.ingramcontent.com/pod-product-compliance
Lightning Source LLC
Chambersburg PA
CBHW040231110526
44582CB00001B/20